I brought you this way only because I wanted you to see the South at its most beautiful: the green sloping campus to the red brick buildings with the tall white porticoes of Washington and Lee University. I wish it were the picture of the South. I wish, indeed, it were the picture of America.
Jonathan Daniels, *Harpers* Magazine, November 1942

The valley of Virginia is a region where a man's
spirit finds broad horizons. No wonder Lexington
was chosen as the site for a college, and no wonder
that that college to this day puts a mark on its
alumni which is as indelible as it is indefinable.
Meredith Nicholson, *A Virginia Impression:*
W & L, 1906

*Its location, its history, its independence and its great
founders seem forever to set the institution apart from
narrow limitations, low aims and sordid labors, to
serve the things of the spirit.*
Calyx, 1925

WASHINGTON

To promote literature in this
rising empire, and to encourage the
arts, have ever been amongst the
warmest wishes of my heart.
And if the donation is likely to
prove a means to accomplish these
ends, it will contribute to the
gratification of my desires.

G. Washington

&LEE

Young gentleman, we have no printed rules. We have but one rule here, and it is that every student must be a gentleman.

R E Lee

Washington and Lee

UNIVERSITY

1749

PHOTOGRAPHY BY WILLIAM STRODE

HARMONY HOUSE

Publishers Louisville

A book in the making requires special care and nurtur-
ing, and the Washington and Lee community has been
bountiful in its help, encouragement, advice, direction
and hospitality. Our very special thanks go to
President John Wilson; project coordinator and
Assistant to the President Frank Parsons; Director of
University Relations Farris Hotchkiss; Associate Dean
of Students Buddy Atkins; Director of University
Publications Jeff Hanna; News Office Director Brian
Shaw; Special Collections librarians Erin Foley
and Lisa McCown; and Public Services and
Reference Librarian Peggy Hayes.

Executive Editors: William Butt and William Strode
Library of Congress Catalog Number 86-081504
Hardcover International Standard Book Number 0-916509-06-0
Printed in USA by Pinaire Lithographing Corp., Louisville, Kentucky
First Edition printed 1986 by Harmony House Publishers-Louisville
P. O. Box 90, Prospect, Kentucky 40059 (502) 228-2010/228-4446
Copyright ©1986 by Harmony House Publishers-Louisville
Photographs copyright© by William Strode

John Robinson Monument

Ah me! How beautifully the South remembers her dead. I have not found in any other statue the noble dignity and sublime peace with which Valentine has touched the outward form of Lee in the quiet chapel at Lexington.

Meredith Nicholson, *A Virginia Impression: W&L,* 1906

INTRODUCTION

White columns and red brick, a footbridge longer than most…dogwood and rosebud in springtime, an autumn blaze of maples and oaks, the occasional white silence of winter… statues, one of standing wood, one of recumbent marble…House Mountain to the west, the majestic Blue Ridge on the eastern horizon.

Some things we share are physical—images as tangible for today's freshmen as they are for our post-war veterans or our octogenarians.

There are, too, abstract threads that bond us— notions, traditions, relationships.

Trusting and being trusted…college friendships…the splendidly redundant exhilaration of winning again, another time…Gilliam, Gaines, Leyburn and other paragons…the cups of knowledge and opportunity, lightly tasted or quaffed, but never drained.

So much that is good and true endures at Washington and Lee that it permits the University to exist apart from time, even as it changes in clearly perceptible ways from one student generation to another. Virtually all the color photographs in this book were made within the past year, yet they span decades in their evocative imagery. So do the words that follow, spoken first to an alumni gathering in 1973 by Sidney M.B. Coulling, professor of English. Like the University itself, like Bill Strode's photographs, his message endures.

Some of my alumni friends who return to campus tell me rather ruefully from time to time that Washington and Lee isn't what it used to be. I must confess that my initial impulse is to ask with what they are comparing it. I've known something of this University during times both of prosperity and of adversity, and its past has never seemed to me a changeless one.

I entered Washington and Lee as a freshman in the fall of 1942 and in the first week of classes lost my instructor in English to the Navy, shortly thereafter lost his successor to the Army when he became Major Frank J. Gilliam, in a few more weeks lost my room in the dormitory to the School for Special Services, and soon after the beginning of the second semester lost my place in the University when, along with one-third of the entire student body, I entered the Army. I returned with that great influx of veterans following the Second World War, and eight years after receiving my degree I came back as a member of the faculty.

When I'm told, therefore, that Washington and Lee isn't what it once was, I'm inclined to ask, "Isn't what it was *when?*" In the thirties, the depression years when faculty salaries were reduced? Or in the early forties,

when the student body dwindled to a tiny group and the University was sustained by the presence of military personnel? Or in the late forties, when veterans came en masse, returning and graduating at so many different times during the year that one lost a sense of the identity of classes or even of the student body as a whole?

But perhaps this is quibbling. All of us cherish memories of our years at Washington and Lee, and if the picture they summon up doesn't correspond to what we observe today we naturally conclude that changes have occurred. But sometimes we revel in sentiment and seek escape from the uncertainties of the present by retreat into the safety of the past. For many of my generation a characteristic recollection of Washington and Lee consists of memories of fraternity parties; of football games at Charlottesville and Charleston; of formal dances culminating in Finals, with Tommy Dorsey, and a crowd seated on the soft grass of the front campus, and the haunting melody of "Green Eyes" gently caressing the warm spring air; of moonlight, and young couples walking hand in hand across the longest concrete non-suspension footbridge in the world. Music, youth, romance—pure nostalgia!

If this is merely a quibble, it is so only to those who refuse to face squarely the real issues in American education today. Washington and Lee, like the rest of the world, *has* changed. The helpful response to this fact, however, is not a lament for times past, but a willingness to understand the changes that have taken place and to make whatever additional changes may be desirable in the future.

Nevertheless, my basic quarrel with the alumni friends to whom I referred a few moments ago is not that they are indulging in nostalgia. My real quarrel is with a kind of hidden assumption that sometime in the past there existed, like an Idea from Platonic thought, an ideal Washington and Lee, and that we have some-how departed from this ideal. The assumption is never explicitly stated, of course, and perhaps it's not even consciously implied. But during the past few years it has made itself so apparent to me that I've been driven to ask what truth, if any, lies behind it. Are we at Washington and Lee, I've asked myself, true to our heritage? Are we indeed helping to realize the aspirations that our predecessors had for this University?

Now when we speak in this manner of our heritage, we're surely speaking of only part of it. I don't think of myself, for example, as an alumnus of Augusta Academy, or of Liberty Hall, or of Washington Academy, or even of Washington College. When we think of ourselves as part of the tradition of this University, we're really thinking of that part of the tradition associated

with Robert E. Lee, with his presidency and the legacy he left. What, then, was Lee's concept of the college he was invited to lead at a most difficult time? What was his attitude toward change, and what were his dreams for Washington College?

In order to have some sense of what the college was like before Lee's presidency, let's consider the catalogue for the session of 1859-60, the last academic year before the Civil War for which a catalogue was published. It's only a slender little pamphlet, but even so its fifteen pages are more than enough to list the names of a faculty of eight and a student body of ninety-five (only one of whom, incidentally, was from out of state), and the courses in a curriculum restricted almost entirely to Latin, Greek, mathematics, the natural sciences, and philosophy.

To turn from this to the catalogue published exactly ten years later, the last year of Lee's presidency, is to enter an altogether new and different era in the history of this University. In the first place the catalogue is no longer a thin pamphlet but a substantial volume five times the length of its predecessor. It lists a faculty that has nearly tripled in size and a student body that has more than tripled; and unlike the provincial student body of 1859, the student body of 1869 represents twenty-two states in addition to the Idaho Territory, Canada, and France.

Such rapid growth in the size and complexity of the student body must surely have raised questions concerning discipline. Lee was a military man, moreover, and one would suppose that under his presidency the students of Washington College were more strictly governed than before. Well, let's turn to the history of those years to see what actually occurred. Let's look at *General Lee's College*, by the late Ollinger Crenshaw. Here is what he writes:

"The shift from rigid rules of discipline to a gentleman's code of conduct was accompanied by a broadening of social life and a relaxation of religious requirements. Dancing became openly countenanced, social fraternities were tolerated, and chapel services were placed on a voluntary basis."

Rules and regulations were relaxed, then, and puritanical restrictions removed. But what about academic and curricular matters? Did they keep pace with a greatly enlarged faculty and student body and with a more sophisticated college life? Lee had come here with limited academic experience, and one might reasonably suppose that he would have been content with the old curriculum. Yet here again he proved himself to be an innovator, dissatisfied with things as they were and eager to meet the challenge of changing times. During the first year of his administration the Lexington Law School was formally annexed to Washington College. A students' business school was established, and practical training of printers and journalists begun. In the spring of 1867 a massive reform of the curriculum was put into effect, adding a number of subjects and creating nine independent departments. Academic standards were raised by the addition of graduate degrees and the creation of the award of "Distinction" for students with outstanding records.

In view of all these changes, which brought to the campus a cosmopolitan student body, created an atmosphere that stimulated a sense of responsibility, and introduced a curriculum designed to meet the different needs of students—with all these changes, can anyone imagine a graduate of Washington College returning to Lexington early in the fall of 1869 and, seeing the institution flourishing as it never had flourished before, remarking nostalgically to General Lee that he certainly missed the good old days?

The question isn't intended to invite comparison with the present times, although the parallel is too obvious to ignore. In certain respects—in cultural advantages, for example, or in diversity of course offerings—the Washington and Lee of today is as much stronger than the Washington and Lee I entered when a freshman, as the Washington College of 1869 was stronger than that of ten years earlier.

Yet the real profit derived from recalling Lee's presidency lies not in drawing parallels but in being reminded that Washington and Lee has never been a static institution, that change is an indispensable part of our heritage. "The atmosphere of Universities," George Meredith wrote almost a century ago in declining an honorary degree from Oxford, "is rather overcharged with the calm Past, and has to be resisted." Washington and Lee's past is one that alumni are justly proud of, but we must resist the temptation to dwell on it except insofar as it gives us renewed appreciation of the motto, rooted deep in the University's history, which proclaims that we are not unmindful of the future.

That future will rest in part on our continuing success in preserving two of the fundamental virtues in our tradition, integrity and civility. But it will rest largely on our ability to perform, in a constantly changing world, the work for which Washington and Lee is primarily intended: awakening, and then helping to gratify, the desire for knowledge and intellectual development. This desire takes many forms, and is satisfied in many ways. But although its expression today may not be precisely the same as in the past, the pursuit of knowledge is our preeminent mission now just as it was in the days of William Graham, and Robert E. Lee, and Francis P. Gaines. No less than in their day, moreover, it is a collective enterprise, and behind it we may all unite as alumni dedicated to advancing the welfare of our University.

— Sidney M.B. Coulling, professor of English

MAJOR DATES IN W&L'S PAST

1914 — Omicron Delta Kappa founded at Washington
         and Lee
1915 — Doremus Gymnasium built with funds donated
         by Mrs. Robert Parker Doremus
1920 — Graham Dormitory built, named for
         William Graham
1925 — Howe Hall built, formerly called the chemistry
         building
1928 — The memorial footbridge to Wilson Field built
1931 — The Wilson Field Stadium completed
1934 — The original Tucker Hall destroyed by fire
1941 — Carnegie Library enlarged and name changed to
         McCormick Library
1941 — Graham-Lees Dormitory completed to
         accommodate freshmen
1942 — The Army School for Personnel Services established
1949 — Bicentennial celebration Washington and Lee
         stamp issued
1950 — *Shenandoah*, a literary magazine, began publication
1954 — duPont Hall erected to house art department
1954 — Athletic grants-in-aid discontinued
1956 — Vice President Alben Barkley's death at the Mock
         Convention in Doremus Gymnasium
1959 — Letitia Pate Evans Dining Hall completed
1959 — The Newton D. Baker Dormitory for law students
         erected
1959 — The John W. Davis Dormitory for upperclassmen
         erected

1961 — New Science Hall constructed; named Parmly
         Hall in 1975
1962 — Gilliam Dormitory built for freshmen
1963 — Lee Chapel restored by Ford Motor Co. Fund
1966 — Alumni House occupied by the Alumni Association
1969 — Early-Fielding University Center opened
1969 — Trustees reorganize: term memberships,
         mandatory retirement age
1971 — Addition to Doremus Gymnasium completed;
         dedicated as Warner Center 1977
1972 — Women admitted to the Washington and Lee Law
         School
1972 — Decade–long development program announced:
         $56 million goal
1975 — Woods Creek Apartments constructed
1977 — Lewis Hall, law complex, dedicated
1979 — New undergraduate library occupied; dedicated
         1980
1980 — McCormick Hall renovated for use of the School of
         Commerce
1981 — Tucker and Newcomb Hall renovated for
         The College
1982 — Reeves Center for Decorative Arts dedicated
1982 — Graham–Lees Freshman Dormitory renovated
1982 — Decade–long development program ends:
         $67 million raised
1984 — Trustees vote to admit undergraduate women
1985 — First undergraduate women enroll

Ruins of Liberty Hall Academy

Cyrus McCormick Statue

You know, as I get older, my definition of the University becomes simpler and simpler. I am at the stage now of believing it to be simply the place where extended conversations take place between and among people with interesting minds.
President John D. Wilson, 1983

But if (the observer) will ascend to the top of one of the university buildings he will behold a landscape which called forth from the lips of the accomplished Professor Farnum the exclamation: "If this scene were set down in the middle of Europe, the whole continent would flock to see it."
William Henry Ruffner, 1893

duPont Hall

Lee Chapel

Doremus Gymnasium

The University Library

*But in the spring! Our young and growing fancies
have turned, not lightly as saith the poet, but heavily,
bodily, totally to thoughts of calic. How could we
help it, with the loveliest of campuses before us, and
the sweetest of maidens strolling so temptingly,
so frequently, so slowly over its beautiful sward?*
B.F. Harlow, '97

Greatness in an institution is difficult indeed to achieve or to maintain. It requires toil and treasure, with no practical or arbitrary limitation upon either. Yet the one indispensable element of greatness — integrity — is available merely by resolution to have it and to keep it.
Dr. Fred C. Cole, Inaugural Address, 1960

Woods Creek

Newcomb Hall

The Co-op

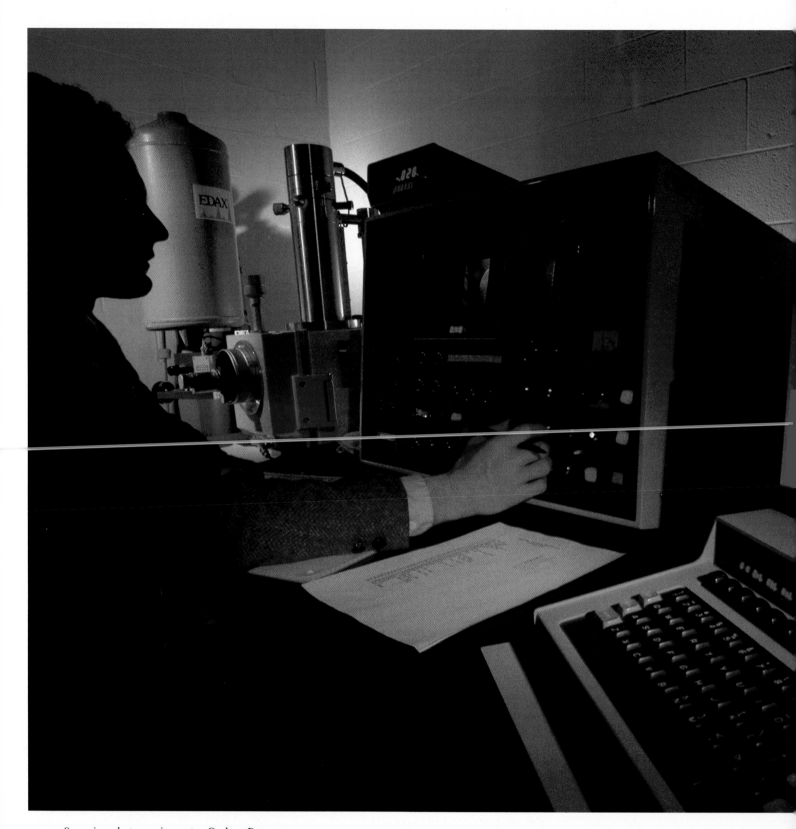

Scanning electron microscope, Geology Department

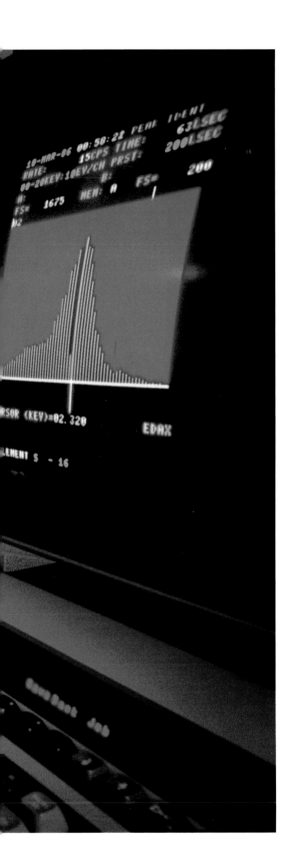

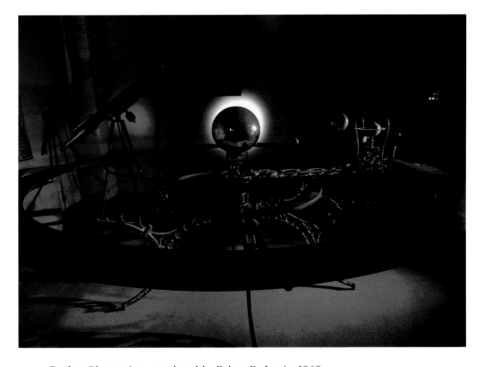

Barlow Planetarium, purchased by Robert E. Lee in 1868

House Mountain

Natural Bridge of Virginia

These are the hills that cradled me and to which as a boy and man I lifted up my eyes for help. Among these now lie those who gave me life, and to whose high precept and example I owe all that have ever been and all that I can hope to be.
John W. Davis, '92, alumni speech in 1924

Goshen Pass

If you close your eyes and conjure up the ideal campus—red brick buildings with rows of white columns, a placid commons beneath the arching branches of ivy-covered trees, a small town of 19th century storefronts—you've got Washington & Lee.
USA Today, 1985

Cadaver Society

Fraternity House

Sigma Society cabin

I have a self-imposed task which I must accomplish.
I have led the young men of the South in battle; I
have seen many of them die in the field; I shall
devote my remaining energies to training young
men to do their duty in life.
Robert E. Lee, 1865

For all its venerable customs, youth is the keynote of the place, and though professors may protest and chaperones may carp, youth continues to have its fling here.
Stuart Moore, 15, in Alumni Magazine, 1925

Fancy Dress

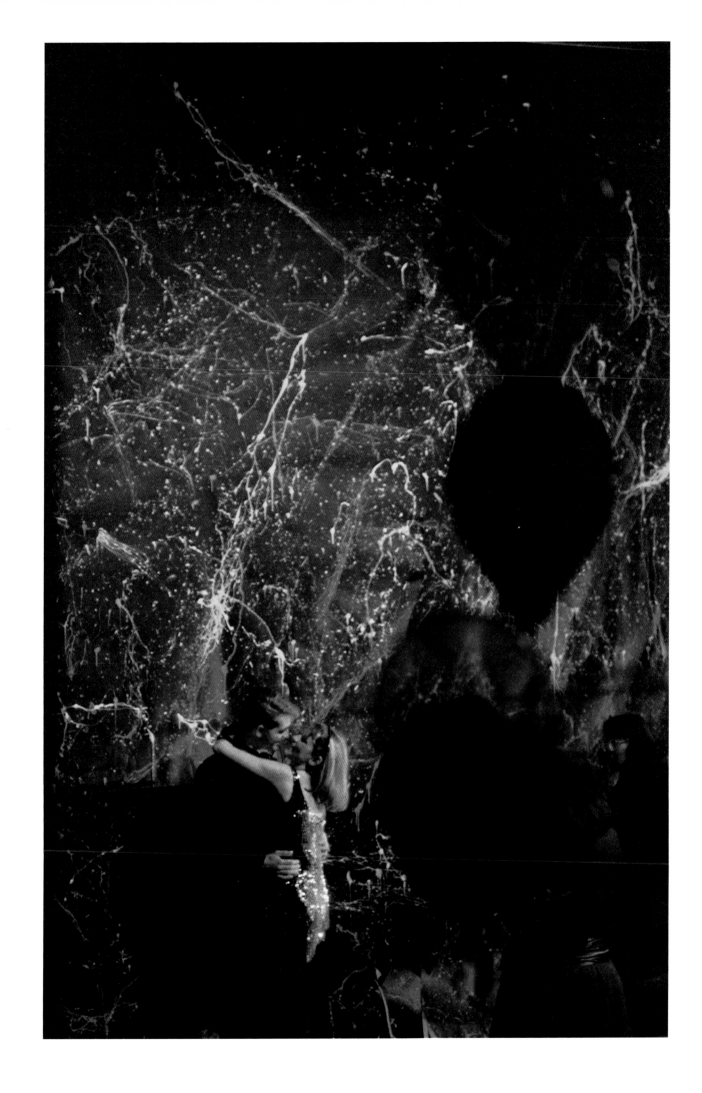

It is a place in which it is still possible to talk of ideals and of courtesy and of civility and even to practice those things.
President John D. Wilson, 1983

Porcelain Collection, Reeves Center

ODK Circle, commemorating the founding of the national honor society on this campus in 1914.

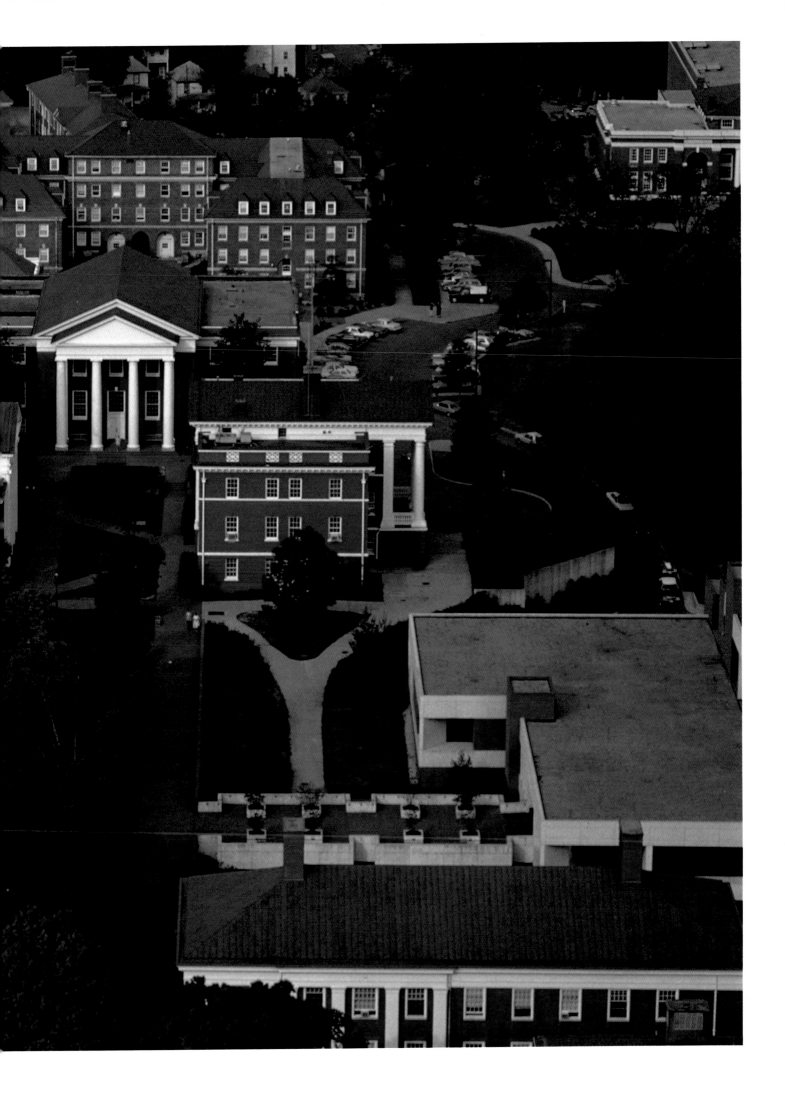

Lewis Hall, School of Law

I have often stopped to think concerning the very small amount of direct moral teaching there was at the university. And yet it is a safe wager that nine out of ten Washington and Lee alumni would say that not even the boyhood years at home were fraught with such impressive lessons in morality. The air at W & L always seemed to me to be one part hydrogen, two of oxygen and three parts ethics. Walter Edward Harris, *The Alumni, Great and Otherwise,* 1937

Wilbur C. Hall Library, School of Law

School of Law

In other words, with its history and traditions and background, Washington and Lee must become the soul of the new South, interpreting the South to itself, conserving the spirit of the past and translating it into the actualities of the present.
Prof. Robert H. Tucker, Acting President, 1930

Lee Chapel

Overleaf: Lee Recumbent Statue by Edward Valentine

Washington and Lee participates in collegiate athletics both on the club level...

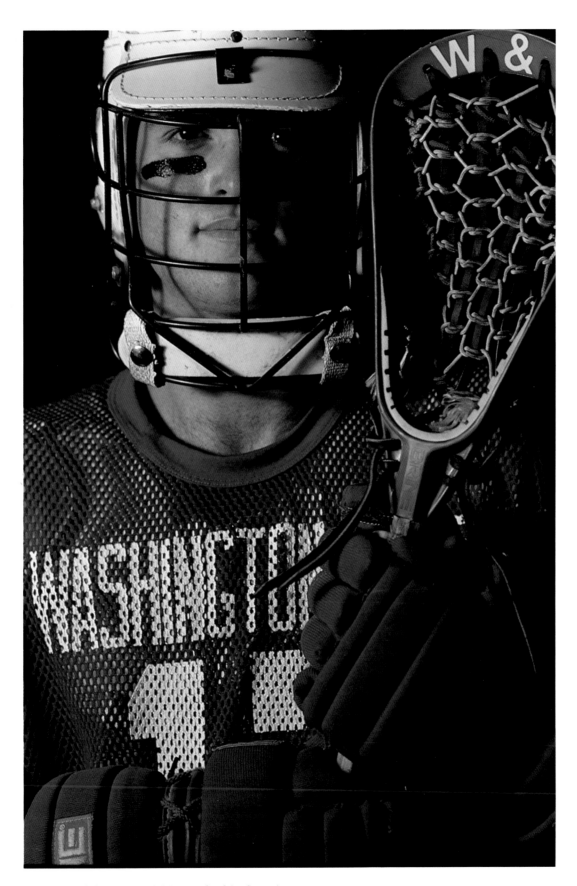

...and the NCAA Division III level in the major sports.

It may not be a Michelangelo creation, but in sentiment and affection of Washington and Lee men it means more than the Winged Victory or the Venus de Milo.
Henry Boley, *Lexington in Old Virginia,* 1935

George Washington statue atop Washington Hall

Overleaf: Baccalaureate service in Evans Hall

Our ceremonies are, I think, symbolic of the character of the place. The beauty of the location, the direct simplicity and almost casual dignity of the proceedings—I like all that. No one else does it quite so well, in my view.
Robert E.R. Huntley, President's commencement remarks, 1982

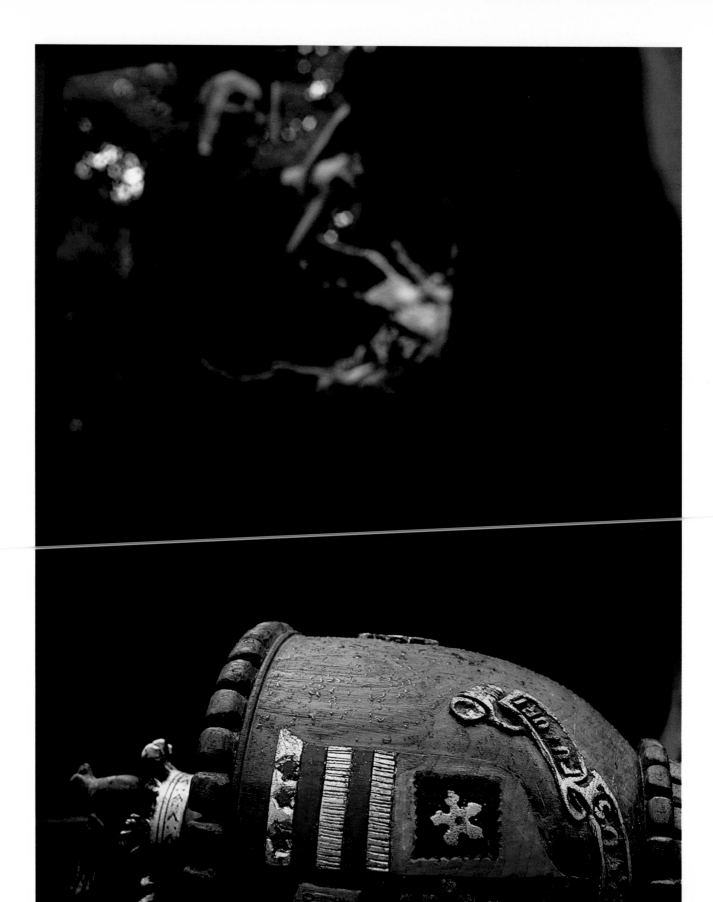

*Around his heart's affections are twined the Alma-
Maternal apron strings, till, when his graduation
day comes, he finds that his home is here, his friends
are here and his treasure and his heart are here.*
B.F. Harlow, '97

*On the campus of the university to which he gave
his last full measure of devotion, his contribution
to the Union, his leadership and integrity are
carried forward in the hearts of your young
students. In the promise of these men, gathered
equally from all parts of the United States, I find
the fulfillment of Lee's career.*
President Dwight D. Eisenhower, on the
occasion of the 150th anniversary of
Robert E. Lee's birth, 1957

Benefactor's Wall, Washington Hall

The photographs in this section have been researched in the Special Collections division of the university library, which contains and administers the Michael Miley Collection and the Rockbridge Historical Society Collection, from which nearly all the photographs were selected.

WASHINGTON and LEE
PHOTOGRAPHS FROM THE PAST

This ambrotype of the Washington College buildings
dates to the late 1850's, and is the earliest-known
photograph of the campus.

The ruins of the forerunner of Washington College, the Liberty Hall Academy, are shown here in the late 19th century, more than 100 years after its final construction on this site in 1793.

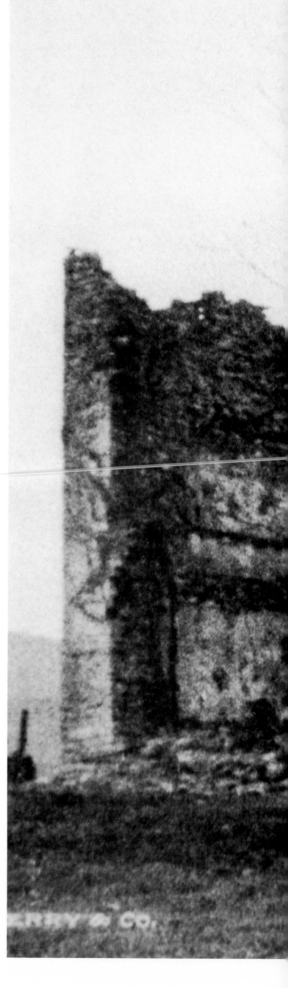

"Removed now by long decades from my own student days, I am frequently impressed by what little memories of that period mean to me. They are more than pleasurable recollection; they are renewals of something I need."
Dr. Francis P. Gaines, 1953

The village of Lexington, circa 1865.

This Michael Miley photograph of Lee was taken
in January, 1870, nine months before his death.

The "new" President's House, constructed for Lee in 1868-69. The three-sided veranda was designed by Lee for his wife, who was crippled with arthritis.

Below, Gen. Lee's office, preserved as he left it, is showcased in the Lee Chapel.

Lee's funeral on Main Street in Lexington,
October 15, 1870.

For three days after Lee's death on October 12, 1870, Lee's body remained in state in the chapel. Washington College students maintained a vigil over his coffin until the burial on October 15.

This famous scene is from the October 15, 1870 funeral of General Lee. Notice the black-draped columns of Washington Hall, then called the Centre Building.

This view of Lee Chapel dates to 1883, the year the Lee Mausoleum was completed on the rear of the chapel building. In this apse lies the Valentine recumbent statue of Lee.

An alumni reunion in 1894.

"Old" Tucker Hall, erected in 1900 for the School of Law, which Lee had incorporated into the college in 1866. This building burned in 1934, and was replaced by "New" Tucker Hall, whose design was more in keeping with the classical style of the early structures.

TUCKER MEMORIAL HALL, WASHINGTON & LEE UNIVERSITY LEXINGTON, VA.

The advent of World War I mobilized W & L students into ROTC units, one of which is shown here, circa 1916.

This Front Campus view is from the 1930's, and shows the relative consistency of the Colonnade since its first construction in the 1820's.

Lexington, circa 1920.

The football team scrimmages in 1890.

The Washington and Lee baseball team of 1914 in action
on its home field, with a capacity crowd.

Washington and Lee's four-man crew on the Maury River in 1891.

he track team in competition, circa 1900.

"Old George", the Mathew Kahle statue, has stood atop Washington Hall since May, 1844. In this picture the statue is shown stripped of nearly a century of paint coatings, just prior to re-painting.

The Reading Room of the Carnegie Library, circa 1935.

U.S. Senator Alben Barkley, the former Vice President, delivers the keynote address to the 1956 Democratic Mock Convention in Doremus Gymnasium. A few moments after the photo was made, he fell dead of a heart attack.

...to think of Washington and Lee is to believe in an ideal...to think of this ideal is to believe that still it has power. Its power is to survive the unforeseen vicissitude, to enlist great teachers, great friends. But more than this, its power is still to achieve a distinctive purpose; to reach beyond the monotony of instruction, beyond the formulas of fact, forever widening and forever intensifying, forever important and forever trivial, to reach beyond these and deposit in the life of a boy something a little finer than culture, a little rarer than competence, a little nobler than success; to quicken a dream within the young brain prepared for dreams by the agony of the aeons, to formulate within the tenderness of the heart some coherence for its own compulsions, to furnish young personality with potency and poise.

Dr. Francis P. Gaines, Inaugural Address, 1930